REBECCA GOSS lives in Suffolk. Her first full-length collection, *The Anatomy of Structures*, was published in 2010 by Flambard Press. Her second collection *Her Birth* (Carcanet/Northern House, 2013) was shortlisted for the Forward Prize for Best Collection 2013, the Warwick Prize for Writing 2015 and the Portico Prize for Literature 2015. It won the poetry category in the East Anglian Book Awards in 2013. In 2014, Rebecca was selected for the Poetry Book Society's Next Generation Poets. *Carousel*, her collaboration with the photographer Chris Routledge, was published in 2018 by Guillemot Press. She has an MA in Creative Writing from Cardiff University, and is currently studying for a PhD by Publication at the University of East Anglia. She is 2018/19 Creative Writing Fellow at Liverpool John Moores University.

REBECCA GOSS

GIRL

CARCANET • Northern House

First published in Great Britain in 2019 by
Carcanet/Northern House
Alliance House, 30 Cross Street
Manchester, M2 7AQ
www.carcanet.co.uk

MIX
Paper from
responsible sources
FSC
www.fsc.org   FSC® C014540

A CIP catalogue record for this book is
available from the British Library.
ISBN 978 1 78410 723 9

Text design by Andrew Latimer
Printed in Great Britain by SRP Ltd, Exeter, Devon

The publisher acknowledges financial
assistance from Arts Council England.

Supported using public funding by
ARTS COUNCIL
ENGLAND

Contents

The Lightning 5

Repossession 7

Girl 9

Ants 11

The Baby Who Understood Shadows 12

Rachel 13

Jogging with Roger 14

The Woman, a Coat and Her Behaviour 15

Fabric 16

Betty Draper Shoots at Her Neighbour's Pigeons 17

I Was Left to Wipe Myself and Dress 18

The Most Beautiful Part of My Daughter 19

Pleurisy I 20

Ida and the Box 21

The Water's Fine 23

Nomenclature 24

With Sarah 26

Bright Celestial Objects 28

Marriage Is a Room of Lit Bulbs 29

Reverse Charge Call 31

Alison 32

Pleurisy II 34

Dare 35

To Say Everything Is White 36

Drinking Their Capri-Suns 37

Well 39

The Certificates 41

White Currants 42

it is still my favourite thing 43

Dodgems 45

Pleurisy III 46

The Vaccination Gymnasium 47
My Sister Has an MRI Scan 48
Your Palm Is a Flag 50
Emprise 51
Talking about the Old House 52
Sebastian and the Fireworks 53
Wet 54
My Husband, Aged Five, Runs the Corridors of His School 55
From Such Folds 56
First Person Narrative 57
Pleurisy IV 59
A Man Sets Down His Secateurs for the Day 60
Collectables 61
To Fall 63
Scabies 65
Pleurisy V 66
Warren Street 67
Something Beautiful Was Created by Their Leaving 68

Acknowledgements 71

GIRL

FOR ROSIE

'As time went on, I found the shape of my life.'

EAVAN BOLAND
from A Journey with Two Maps: Becoming a Woman Poet

The Lightning

First, it split a tree.

Then tripped across a barbed wire fence
as my mother watched, thrilled.

It entered through her feet. Threw her
ten yards onto grass, where it briefly

stopped her heart, burnt nerves,
fused her jaw and exited through her mouth.

She tells me this, countless times
and each time I see her, jerking

on the ground, stricken with volts,
her mouth spitting rods of light.

She had to re-learn writing, walking,
reading, speaking but eventually

repaired to have me; let me float
in the bowl of her womb, only to be born

and find her wheelchair bound.
Blood vessels of each foot destroyed,

her ten toes finally gone. I grew up
in the seat of her lap. Once level with her throat,

I strained to see inside her mouth,
find its trembling, silver pool.

Tonight, her bedtime whispers feel fiery
in my hair and when she thinks I'm sleeping,

I'm half-hidden in my doorway, watching her
glide back down the landing,

all her fingers trailing sparks.

Repossession

'Did you buy apples?' I look at our replenished bowl
and you describe the last house of the day.

Taps strangled with tape, tank drained, letterbox sealed.
The debris of hurried exits – one trainer, scattered CDs,

pens, cheap clothes and a last bin liner, too heavy
and cumbersome, its pan handles poking through the skin.

There's the damage, more than a few scuffs on magnolia,
today a radiator ripped out in rage, but it's the kids' toys

that get to you. Outside, about to plot the boundary,
you'd forgotten how hot it was and loosened your tie,

freed the heat collecting at your neck. Unusual to see a tree
in the gardens of this street, yet there it was, beckoning

with a branch of red globes. The rest you say quickly –
that you would never take something normally,

but you knew it would be unoccupied for some time,
it seemed wasteful to leave them, rotting in the sun.

I picture you scrumping in a suit. Jacket unbuttoned,
brogues close to the trunk, a toe dipping in fruity mulch,

disturbing a wasp's boozy crawl, your awkward stretch
to save the last dozen from their fate. I keep thinking

what would I leave if we had to surrender our home,
filter its contents fifteen years deep? I take hold of your hand,

say 'It's okay, I'll wash them.' We eat them in a week,
swiping from the bowl, twisting their woody stalks as if they're
    really ours.

Girl

after Alison Watt 'Hollow' (2009)

An opening: marquise cut,
determining how my mother

would dress me,
how she would tip my head

towards the world,
tell me I was a beautiful thing.

Its evolution was slow.
The pale plum of myself, visible

on lawns of a childhood
until I grew to recognise

its very private reek,
found it capable of quiver, stretch.

A finger's hook at cotton seams,
how that push inside

could change me. It's where
I felt the water, first time

I chilled myself in sea.
But for heat, that would take you

to lie down at its haw, cause
a tipping to begin —

a somersaulting into love
that made a daughter.

And I'll tell her,
it's where they looked first —

eyeing through my squall and kick
to identify me as girl.

Ants

They came for us as we breathed – unified and quivering
on blond gymnasium ash. Eager elbows of antennae

in a dark, tremulous lace as fourteen pregnant women
lay beached on Pilates mats. A midwife's sudden alarm

at the trembling, advancing line but her panic was rebuffed
in a sports hall of barn proportions. We simply moved our mats

to start again, sprawled ourselves like snails. You stirred at this,
a prod of confirmation, and I held my belly like a ready pear.

Opening an eye, I glimpsed the odd brave stray, its glossy nodes defined,
now free of the pack. I was squeezing my pelvic floor when they muscled

their way under and with one collective heave lifted me, inches
from the ground. Hard to believe I didn't smash their shiny backs

as they marched me one triumphant lap, past the cracked heels
of tired, expectant women. As we headed for the door, I'm sure

I heard you laughing, felt you leap in me like mischief,
your mother superbly weightless, on a sheet of shivering black.

The Baby Who Understood Shadows

She found him, on his front, one arm raised
and conducting the air. Three months old,

his limbs mere feelers on her carpeted home,
until the sun tipped his shadow on the floor:

made a shape impossible to push or pull
and he acted upon it. She believed

he was reaching, that his fingers
wanted to grab, but the shadow

was all there was, dancing
beneath his elbow. He hadn't heard her

come into the room, hadn't flexed
to her milky scent. She watched

as the link between light, object, surface
became coherent to this speechless being.

His eyes followed fist. The fist she held
in her lips, when love required her to eat him

in mouthfuls. This baby she washed, fed,
kept close as fog, now able to see through

the branches of her arms, find the sun's rays,
his own shadow, all things that are not her.

Rachel

I spent the day being Rachel. I introduced myself as Rachel
to a stranger at the library, when we reached for the same copy
of *The New Encyclopedia of Birds*. I apologised in a way Rachel

would have apologised: prone to genuflection.
I let him take the book and wedge it under his armpit
so he could bend for his umbrella, just as I was telling him

my name was Rachel, but he turned and headed for the Loans desk.
I decided that as Rachel, I wasn't interested in birds after all,
and anyway, I didn't have a library card signed by Rachel

in black felt-pen, so I hit the big, circular button with a picture
of a wheelchair on it and waited for the doors to open fully.
I walked around the town, in rain that fell as if it was undecided

about its volume. Scant bursts would be the best way
to describe it, had someone telephoned, and after I'd said
Hello, this is Rachel speaking, told them about the weather.

Jogging with Roger

He likes the choreography: how they convene
for synchronised stretching before pounding in tandem,
all set to the reassuring bounce of their cocks.

The talk is of money and risk, money and luck
and though he never looks at his longtime neighbour,
he knows Roger is sweating, his face turning puce.

Roger doesn't know the details of his life:
that he thinks about sex most of the day, will return home
to shower, wear yesterday's shirt, smell the tang

of his assistant, still on his cuff. He wonders if Roger
likes to taste sweet, weak women; if Roger has secrets too.
He thinks about Julia, staked on a lounger, honeying

her limbs, how he pretends not to notice Roger's
spectacular wife. They circle the oak on Oak Tree Drive,
pant the last stretch home, their finish rewarded

by the first glare of sun. As they bend to grip knees
he notes their heavy watches, the year round tan to their arms
but it's the ring of grey, sticky on Roger's scalp

that renders him stricken, knowing it mirrors his own,
leaves him wheezing on concrete in another day's light.

The Woman, a Coat and Her Behaviour

I spot her trying on the coat from the far end
of the shop. She's doing what normal women do –
turning a little this way, a little that way, in a swing
of black ribbon and felt. Her slim wrists slide
into pockets and her head tilts back to catch
her husband's smile. She laughs at her own behaviour.

If customers knew she had a son wasting in a hospital,
would they approve of this coquettish dance? Parents
of the almost-dead cannot always be bed-side, reverent
and mute. This small act affirms what they had,
when a telephone call from their son was enough.
Let her arms fill the sleeves of a beautiful coat
before she delivers clean pyjamas, leans to kiss
a dumb mouth and carousels his life, from baby to boy.

Fabric

after Alison Watt, 'Black Star' (2012)

I woke alone,
and searched for you
where I thought the heat of us
might be clouding
in that yawn of fabric,
my fingers pushing into its slate dark –
back into our universe of night
when you gathered the whole of me
and I pulled you under –
so we could explode everything cold
or white about this space
until the breath we had
came out as flares
and I was the one to surface

Betty Draper Shoots at Her Neighbour's Pigeons

Gone noon, in ivory nightgown,
one Lucky Strike jutting
from her mouth, she tips up the gun

and aims at their swooping grace.
The crack that comes
rouses the man who threatened

her children's dog, his remaining birds
now panicked in their cage.
She keeps firing, sheer sleeves

slipping to her elbows, and maybe
there's a shot in there for husband
Don, his absences at night.

Maybe a shot for motherhood too,
and the era that keeps her
like a butterfly, pinned in the home

with her rioting young. The hours
of dishes, laundry, all of it accomplished
with that silent, divine face.

On a perfect lawn, glossed nails
on the trigger, Betty Draper
shoots at her neighbour's pigeons

and she's smoking the whole time.

I Was Left to Wipe Myself and Dress

after Bruce McLean, 'Hot Slick' (1989)

On my computer screen, a wedge
of purple, the bright disc of sun.
Outlines of bodies traced into paint:
limbs, breasts, the modest placing
of hands over cunts. First real McLean
I saw was at the Women's Hospital,
donated to a waiting room wall,
its vivid canvas obscured by plastic plants.
I had to poke my way through
to check his name in slanted scrawl.
Then my name was called, legs soon captive,
splayed for colposcope and glove.
The sharp delve, in search of abnormality,
all the time being told to relax. Then it was done.
I was left to wipe myself and dress. Sent back
through that room of knowing women,
my head rampant and full of colour.

The Most Beautiful Part of My Daughter

is not what I expected it to be.

She has sated my narcissistic want
for lips to mirror mine, she has

the exact same straightness of hair.
It is near the knuckle of her right hand

that I am drawn to. Her little finger's nub,
fringed by minuscule dots of brown.

Freckles not there at birth, I am sure of it.
They came perhaps two years later,

when my head was turned by work,
and remained unnoticed

until she rested a dripping palm
on the side of the bath.

How did they come, these sweet explosions
on her skin? This constellation.

How did I not hear its boom?
She laughs now when I kiss them,

and as I guide her across roads, fields,
the path to and from school,

I feel them, celestial co-ordinates,
charting themselves in my clasp.

Pleurisy 1

At its most acute,
she pictured an orb,

phosphorescent,
in a snare of rib.

It eased to the pressure
of a handstand,

executed
by someone fully grown

on her chest,
and every cough

discharged small bombs
across her back.

In her most breathless
state, there was a tree –

cankerous and scratching,
malevolent in its reach

around her frame.
She wanted it uprooted,

hauled outside her body,
just to pick off the lungs

snagged amongst branches.

Ida and the Box

When the artist Marc Chagall escaped Nazi-occupied France
in 1941 and sailed for America, it was his daughter Ida who
ensured the collection and safe passage of her father's paintings.
It is believed that for her separate and entire journey by sea, she
sat on the huge box which stored them.

Ida, with your six hundred kilos
of gathered Chagall; passengers stare

at your straight back, your flat palms
pressing on the crate. Behind you,

there is fire. Not smouldering in hearths
but started in homes, to raze them.

This crossing of frontiers brings you
to sit on a box, lashed to the deck,

your haul guarded and close.
Thank God, because you weren't to know

the hold was already damp, rotting
its contents to an insanitary state.

Brooklyn Port Authorities would enter
its stench, throw everything overboard.

Waves pick up the hull, urge this passage on.
You can hear *The Acrobat* tumbling,

the green head of *The Poet*
revolving with ideas. You listen for the swish

of your parents in flight,
The Birthday kiss, where your life

germinated in a posy's spray. Ida,
with your body's freight of water and bone.

Push down, keep still, these animals
and angels you have tamed into dark.

The Water's Fine

He watches her back, pearly
and exposed, because of those

backless costumes she likes, cut
to the very bottom of her spine.

The line of her jaw is sharp
above her shoulder, her body

making amatory twists.
Then she drops from sight

and he runs to the edge of the pool.
Nothing about her is real.

She is submerged, curving,
unable to hear him shouting.

They're still a little drunk.
He isn't sure when this physical

ease between them will stop. Suddenly,
fucking feels the same as drowning.

She appears like a seal, her face sheening,
and swims towards his feet.

'Come in,' she says. 'The water's fine.'

Nomenclature

for Dr *Rebecca Goss*, Professor in Organic/Biomolecular
Chemistry, University of St Andrews

How long did we look at our mothers
from the safe ledge of their hips,
hear the word *Rebecca* spoken, whispered,
(all that soothing, pointing)
until eventually its hard end-vowel
caused the turn of our heads?
Loved for its length, something to offset
our surname's syllabic lack, it suited us.
We were firstborns. We were Rebeccas.
We grew our hair long and straight.
With eager grips on Berol, this shared appellation
practised on pages of feint-rule; school
shaping us into very different women.
In Chemistry, your teacher made sugar syrup
for his bees, you witnessed the substances
of which matter is composed. Science
declared itself to you. Me, I was a smoker,
occasional truant, but really a good girl,
unable to resist when a teacher placed Faulkner
in my hand. I'm ahead of you by two years,
reached certain freedoms and discoveries earlier.
University. Motherhood. I got to sign
our name inside the covers of slim books.
You weren't far behind me, on dance floors
that stirred you until late, with lovers,
knowledge forming its ziggurat in you.
What do I really know of this?

I know your daughter raised her head
when she was born, locked eyes with you in a stare
as you held her shining, intended body.
I know because you wrote it down,
out of all the things you could have told me
and knowing it has made me realise
what we both have,
finds me turning back to reach for you.

With Sarah

We headed for Kenwood House,
walking very close to each other, the way
women can. We lay on the grass, looked back
at the south façade, that wide bank of lawn,
children running its irresistible slope.

I talked for a long time, about sad things.
You responded with those pauses
you are capable of, as if a web is breaking
between your lips just before you speak,
but it means you've heard everything I've said.

We didn't stray to the woods, or come across
the Hepworth, slide our arms through a gash in stone.
We stayed on that grass. And beyond us,
pregnant pipistrelles hung in their summer roosts,
wings folded around gestating pups.

I don't remember leaving the heath, our return
to Brixton. I don't remember my further stretch
back North, to marriage. Years later,
you went to Bahrain, to witness the curbed
liberties of others. I was proud of you

working in a place I didn't know or understand.
But you felt only guilt in the hotel pool,
your body breaking the water's warm surface
of leaves and flowers while your family slept
three thousand miles from your touch.

Perhaps swimming will always make you
think of them, think of the day you breathed and paced
around your flat; lowered your swell into a blue
plastic pool, the relief of water at the split of you,
before the baby rushed. I met him, your first child,

at the funeral of mine, on that hot walk
from the church to my house and I grabbed you
and kissed you and kissed him, but couldn't talk.
Then there was last month, beside you again,
watching my daughter, your sons, curious

at the Horniman museum, their small fingers
pointing to exhibits, choosing to stroke an eagle
and a mole, as we stood behind them, guardians
of coats. After lunch, we took them to fly kites.
Let them run in open space, bright flapping

far above their heads; and it felt as if I'd always been
heading to that point, to be with you in the park,
watching our children cast themselves into flight.

Bright Celestial Objects

after Alison Watt, 'Venus' (2015)

Their backs against the grass,
she felt a pull, as if the leaves

on the trees were lodestones,
the hairs on her skin rising at once.

They reached for each other's fingers,
succumbing to the lift

that took them above crowns of oak,
all the way to the cumulus.

How lost they got, inside the billow,
reaching through white –

their arms slippery with moisture.
Then out, soaring

towards bright celestial objects,
their skins coupling, lucent,

as she looked at him to say
I told you it would be like this.

Marriage Is a Room of Lit Bulbs

For the first year, each touch
remains an illumination.

They speak in sentences
bearing an intensity of light.

The space swells with a child.
A newborn fist uncurls, tips

a brilliance on the floor
and they bathe in it.

Love stretches itself out
to reach everyone in the room.

Unnoticed, a corner dims.
Still the exchanges are sweet, bright,

until fatigue brings a blackout.
Candles give a different hue,

cause a much wanted current:
while the baby sleeps, they lie

beside each other and pulse.
But this is not repeated.

Bulbs are not replaced.
Today, she wakes, dresses

in the shadows. A child cries
and she does not go to him.

There's a sharp sound,
a filament giving out, pop

follows pop, a series of small explosions,
as she makes her way to the door.

Reverse Charge Call

What we girls knew of emergency was slight but peril was waiting. Brown Owl led us to a strip of telephone boxes to demonstrate her wiseness, and the art of a reverse charge call. Redirected to our mothers in that practice run, we offered up the digits learnt for the task – operator confirming connection – our rescue by vibration and wire. The double rings released from that GPO rotary dial, my mother's thirty-year-old hand lifting its curve from the cradle, the syllables of my name falling against her face. I can't recollect a conversation. Doubt there was given time. But What If that call had been redirected to my grown-up self? The operator asking me to accept the sound of me, standing on a pavement in Essex in the 1980s, striving for a badge for my mother to sew to my sleeve. I'd be holding the receiver, decades ahead, proficient in hurt and living, hanging on to my girl-voice, unsure whether to take this one chance and hurl warning.

Alison

You saw her in New York. Not someone like her,
with similar head-tilt, same hair,
cut to be curled behind an ear. No,

it was her. And the bar you both stood in
you can describe to me now,
along with what you were wearing,

what she was wearing. Twenty-two
years later, these are details
that have stored in you like bees.

A radio programme on mistaken identity
disturbs them and I watch you,
home from work, leaning at the sink, telling me

how others have seen not doppelgänger
but husband, wife, brother, returned to them.
How it is momentary, but real.

She'd been gone less than a year,
it was your first trip away from the children,
from the city she died in. You didn't know

what to wear, what to pack. It wasn't a good time
to recklessly get on a plane.
Your lawyer stood on your doorstep,

night before the flight, made you sign a will
because family had become a vulnerable concept.
It was as if she knew the effort it had taken

for you to get there, to grin amongst friends,
and she wanted to buy you a drink at the bar.
Lift a glass of some strong, dark spirit

and nod, as if to say I know you did everything,
you did everything you possibly could.
And look down at your much-needed cigarette,

over your shoulder at the bar's open door,
New York waiting to eat up your sadness
and she saw that widowhood would not

define you. Saw your flight home.
Saw me, holding her children's hands.

Pleurisy II

She tried to cancel out

one great sensation
with another –

wanting the weight of him
to counter

what she felt
and as he held her,

flooding her body
with touch –

cautiously urgent
as she tilted for his push,

hurt bloomed
between her shoulders

and it was
the brightest flowering.

Dare

My jacket open, the cold air hitting me
like a punch.

The park deserted,
the aim to get to the lake
before they do: the other girls

with their lean brown legs
& experienced mouths,

who know about the guises of wolves
& girls like me
unfamiliar with night.

Who won't believe I can scale
locked gates, run past what skulks

beneath swing & slide.
That I can get to the lake,
shake my hair down

before they swarm, their breathlessness
coming at me in clouds.

To Say Everything Is White

after Alison Watt, 'Drift' (2015)

To say everything is white
is to ignore

the grey, black and yellow
in the strokes

and the tides that come,
as you study the bloom.

I have been caught
in the sail of it, plunged downward

and tossed up, no rope.
I've held pearls in my mouth,

felt large, planetary
and I have seen myself, split.

Drinking Their Capri-Suns

There was something infantile about it,
those pouches held in the tender grips

of middle-aged men, a thin orange spike
firm between their lips. They talked

between sucks as if it was the right
beverage aboard a train on its way out

of the city. An impulse purchase perhaps
at the station, their mouths claggy with

motes of the underground, or did they take
from the multi-pack of Suns in the kitchen cupboard,

slip one each into the pockets of their dark
waxy jackets before leaving the house?

I watch them through a gap between seats,
realising I've never tasted a Capri-Sun.

Artificial juice banished from my youth,
and even at 18, with all the permissions

that number granted, I did not buy one.
Nor did I look closely at such men (back then,

I'd have been so sure they were looking at me)
but in these new and unseen times I find myself

taken with their exchange. The punctuation
of its flow comprising not just laughter, much

earnest nodding, but the swallowing of citrus slosh.
If I had one of those shining supple purses

I might think to rise from my seat.
Unbutton my coat. Join them.

Well

Alfredo Rampi (b. 11 April 1975) was an Italian
child who died after falling into a well in Vermicino,
a village near Frascati, 13 June 1981.

He was my age.
I can still see myself
standing in the doorway
as if to get close
to the screen would
have been dangerous,
would have been to peer
over the lip itself.
I watched
the eventual haul
of his dirty body,
how it flopped
as he was carried.
I grew up petrified
of wells. Now, when
parenthood feels like
my only risk,
the story comes back.
What sound did he make?
That widening
of his vocal tract,
a loud vowel,
and his mother so far.
She didn't know her son
had tumbled beneath her
and even if she did, had run

to flatten her chest
on dusty ground, reach
into the black,
what good could it have done
to hear him reversing his birth,
his nails at the roundness -
nothing like his early claw
from her sides, his howl
in a warmer stream.

The Certificates

Mothers were not given space to write their occupations on UK birth certificates until 1984. Source: General Register Office

The registrar takes his pen, tips its freight
of permanent ink to write *Poet* in the space
that did not exist beside my mother's name,

or my grandmother's name. Those bloody,
sweat-drenched women sent back to hearth
and cradle, their skills cancelled, never known.

My mother had four children in a decade,
each certificate proving nothing but birth.
My lineage? Patriarchal: *father/farmer,*

father/journalist, a family's passage from land
to desk, but my mother's story of travel,
of being photographed, of earning in a day

what my father brought home in a week
was hushed. I watch the registrar write,
as my baby daughter cries at my chest,

and I'm thankful for her ringing lungs, this
primary deed, this sure beginning of her archive.

White Currants

The colander, tight in your grasp,
is filled with picked currants. Black-buttoned,
where they tore from the stem,

snipped from inside a wilting shrub
and tumbled against steel sides.
I set one on your tongue. You spit

and shake your head, put the colander down
preferring to pick one for yourself,
turn it, until it bursts in curious fingers.

Your birth is a sharp kick in my brain:
its beginning this time three years ago,
the speed of it, my hushed thrill

at your sex. Today, daughter,
you are stretched with importance:
reaper of bright spawn,

until the colander tips in tired hands
and I lift you, your bare legs closing
at my hip: a harvest of berries and child.

it is still my favourite thing

for J & R

When you see the child I feed, hold
and steer towards her seventh year,
such tasks are not new to me.

I tell you I have stepchildren
but the fact they can't be seen, here at the swings,
means they're too far to seem real.

Rather than persist with the complex story
of how I came to love them,
I'll take you on a necessary quest into the city –

going underground and over, heading east
into the bustle, to see their beautiful liberated limbs
so far from playgrounds now.

I was not the vessel for their birth so their beauty
is a thing I can unashamedly announce.
They flourished from the mould of their mother,

what they gleaned from her features clear enough
to catch their father's breath. Perhaps
there is too much to explain, how I have these

young adults in my life, that I was present
for every single day they went to school.
But I want you to notice them –

the way they brush against each other
as they talk, and it is still my favourite thing,
to see them emerge in the grown shape

of their bodies, at ease in this city's crowds,
waving and walking towards me.

Dodgems

I've come to heighten the present,
throw my body into accident.

A sea of psychedelic skiffs
to choose from and once inside

I brace, await the shock of launch.
Dad and boy are bullied backwards

by larger, louder men. Hooks spark
the ceiling's grille. Hit side-on,

girls scream. This is fairground
din and babel, with music bucking

in my gut. I'm knocked, shunted
to the side, upper body in metronomic

sway. He comes, with ethereal descent,
swooping from bumper to bumper,

hand on the pole, arms all muscle
and inky stain. The answer to peril: seraph

in ripped jeans, he spins me out on the black
expanse so I'm shrieking and conductive.

Pleurisy III

8am – 1g paracetamol
9am – 400mg ibuprofen (with food)
12noon – 1g paracetamol
3pm – 400mg ibuprofen (with food)
4pm – 1g paracetamol
8pm – 1g paracetamol
9pm – 400mg ibuprofen (with food)

The Vaccination Gymnasium

I hold my baby, lift up her chin. Two squirts,
each nostril. She cries. And that should be all.
I should be done with it. Her face buried in my neck

as I grapple her freshly immunised squirm
but it feels like something unexplained
has brought my town together. The elderly,

alphabetised in queues, tip back their heads
in obedience and I'm thinking
this limited natural light is stopping us

from understanding a cloud has become
cyclonic. That it's sucking up from the river
the seven cygnets born this summer.

Horses, cows all scooped inside its core,
twisting over meadow, up the hill to school,
until one person senses a shift in noise and smell,

runs to crash shut the gymnasium doors, while
others follow: a quantity of men, keeping their
bodies hard, braced against the smashing of hooves.

My Sister Has an MRI Scan

for Katherine

Later, she will tell me that she slipped off
her wedding ring for the first time,

left it at home, drove thirty miles
to undress, leaving only her knickers

under the slit robe, and her shoes on.
I'm at my desk, researching everything

I didn't ask her. The vessel, intergalactic
in design, its measured draw

to pull the body in. Radiographer
in a different room, just her

inside a tunnel of magnetic field
and radio waves. She'll wear headphones.

Classical music is common,
but she'll tell me hers were faulty

and the sound was like the reverb
of an amp. I wonder if her eyes will be closed

or open. How she will relent to stillness,
to lying down alone. I want it to be over

and the sheet of findings be printed out,
blank. Or, if that monitor picks up anything,

it is her brain recalling the chill of sea,
the tear of her son's birth: proof her nerves

are living. I want to be there when she sits up,
to grip her arms and receive her.

Your Palm Is a Flag

after Alison Watt, 'Flexion' (2003)

Your palm is a flag
above heads of others
so I can locate the square of this earth
where you stand
and I nod, raise my arm.
We converse by stretch of limb.
As I nudge past shoulders
towards you, a recent morning
comes clear in my mind, when
I broke open the curtains
reachable with an outstretched
hand from our bed, the damp transfer
of condensation revealed, obscuring
our view of the walnut tree.
One night's humidity
declaring itself.
Droplets on cold glass – proof
of temperature, pressure, touch
(all things we have
known each other by)
causing the angles
of our sleepy bodies to contract,
a reluctance
to be upright, or
tall as you are now
in this crowd, beckoning.

Emprise

For years, Italian designer and architect Ettore Sottsass
photographed every hotel room in which he had slept
with a woman. Source: Design Museum, 2015

Was she bathing
as you raised the lens?

Was it a light
you sought before

or afterwards?
Was it the whole room

or just a part of it?
A corner

where desire
became unfastened –

that conscious
shift

into private behaviours.
And you,

wanting to chronicle
intimacy –

how the dawn motes
circled

with her scent.

Talking about the Old House

We're thoughtful
when you mention
the old house, the back bedroom,

how you remember a prolonged phase
of intimacy in that room.
How we carried the blanket
from our own bedroom,
laid it down
and stayed for several months,

content with painted floorboards
and broken sash.
No belongings,
we went in there to flee.

Each night tracing
the sharp relief of my hip.
A pinned-up sheet
barely hiding the moon.

The rest of the house
forsaken to its ghosts.

Sebastian and the Fireworks

for my nephew

I stand beside your mother's stretched belly
and imagine your response to these explosions.
Do you quiver – timid, curled – or star and wheel
in your own black sky? Such electric blooms
above the village green. Is this blaze enough
to register on your pale, closed lids? Your thumb
perhaps a comfort, as you tremble inside
your mother, a family eager to know your shape
and name, as we wait for you, this spark-filled night.

Wet

You remember a sensation of warmth,
but because of obedience, fear

and the fact that you were four, remained
cross-legged on classroom carpet,

whilst feeling the flood in your navy tights.
A dark island spread beneath your knees,

seeped beyond the patent leather toes
of Mary Janes, and around you a slight

shuffling began. Your eyes stayed down
as a teacher's voice rose. Don't you wish

you could go back to that room, kneel beside
that sorry child, absolve her from her sodden lap?

My Husband, Aged Five, Runs the Corridors
of His School

You lie on your back, one hand on my hip,
an absent-minded resting of your palm
and tell me about a day when, overwhelmed
by your stammer, the shrill impatience of nuns,

you fled your desk to run the corridors of your school.
You were chased, could hear Sister Kevin's caw
but kept running, through the Juniors' door, scanning
each class for your sister's face until you found her,

her mouth agape as you clutched her arm, grey socks sunk
to your shins. You can't remember what happened next.
Our daughter stirs and you rise to greet her, the story
falling from our bed. The morning now given to slow

tasks as you dress her in navy; lift satchel, scarf,
kneel down to close the buttons of her coat.

From Such Folds

after Alison Watt, 'Slip' (2015)

From such folds
came my infant.
Vernixed imp,
angry as a storm –
tamed by milk
and the safe plain
of a mother's skin.
Her push against
the seam, her
instigation of the flood,
until it all broke
open and she was
shivering, extant.

First Person Narrative

These leaves are feverish,
agitated by my clamber
and I'm hidden inside the tree,
the depth of its dark a comforting thing –
trying not to look at the lit shape of house
where he might take hours
to understand he doesn't hear me
moving between rooms
and eventually his search will take him to the garden
where I will have already felt
for wide circumference,
healthy limb (just my luck to tie
to something rotted, unreliable)
and whatever sound I make he does not hear it,
only later sees the branch
capable of bearing a fast,
dropped, calamitous weight.

*

Wisp, thought of.
Came when we had
forgotten you were wanted.
Brought joy, brought storms.
Tethered, you persisted.
Then a formation of clouds.
Your skin, mottling.
This lack, aperture,
we snatch at it.

*

See how he touches
the fabric at my waist,
the way it gathers
and he feels the size of me, the delicacy
as I whisper things
to make him throw back his head
and laugh at the new sky above us
with everyone watching,
wanting us to carry on
with this intoxicating
notion of promise.
Look at us dancing.
We know nothing.
We knew nothing at all.

Pleurisy IV

'When doctors listen to the breath, that's what they want
to hear: an openness connecting breath to the sky...'
— Gavin Francis, Adventures in Human Being

She did not spill sky.
Did not open her mouth
and release a piece of firmament.

Something billowed, yes.
It wanted to get out, but its way
was met with rub and thwack.

She dreamt of grace, of breeze.
Taking her out of this bed, and up.

A Man Sets Down His Secateurs for the Day

removes the mud from his shoes, walks the hallway
of his house in yellow tartan socks. In the front room
he lies on the floor, felled by loneliness as if it were a gas.
In this room he painted the walls, raised children; often lit fires,
read books. His first wife never knew this room, but his second
loved to toe the buttons of the Chesterfield when they talked.
Her lean, freckled arm stretched along its back like she was bathing.
The chandelier above him glints. He imagines its plunge,
his sparkling guts skewered to the rug. Then the wives,
fraught at the door with old keys, come to pick out the glass,
hold his head with bloody fingers. All the time whispering
they're sorry, mouthing the names of his children like prayer.

Collectables

It's as if the black opening of the loft
consumes him. The soles of his shoes

disappearing. She's never asked
if he has a seat up there, given himself

some perch before dipping into
each box and, with a tenderness

that she has no doubt would surprise her,
lift something collectable from its set.

She's seen him wrap. She knows the time
he spends on that, so to unwrap must be

a thing of tension. The cautious hulling,
until a glass rolls into his palm.

Eighteenth century makes up the bulk,
an assortment of baluster dram and

engraved flute. He likes detail, stippling.
The way a fingertip can sweep inside.

Yet all of it is viewed under a 60-watt glow,
not in daylight, not in a garden, not in blaze.

The sun upon a slender, composite stem
would be breathtaking, surely. Maybe he considers

the pierce too great, the reflected spangle
a threat upon his clasp. And of course

she would be out there, watching. Neglected
curio, with these new blonde streaks in her hair.

To Fall

is to tangle yourself
in a child's limbs,

as you walk along
a coastline promenade

holding her hand
but then smash

to the ground,
the noise of her head

hitting concrete
troubling you still,

as does your knee's
plum-coloured scar,

the daily feel for its ridge –
after all that blood,

the rip in your dress
and the crying

that went on for days
because it was August.

A month laden with
upsetting dates and to fall

on the day that followed
the anniversary

of your other child's death,
when you were trying

to prove recovery
and control, but instead

pulled your daughter
into harm, meant

you continued to the sand,
bleeding into shoes

and a summer of anxiety
came rushing at you in waves.

Scabies

We holidayed through its incubation.
Time spent with family, the large, extended
swell of us in a rented house by a winter sea.

What we shared that Christmas would burrow
into our warm and secret places, causing us
to begin a new year baffled by scratching.

The yo-yo trips to doctors, all those different creams
for eczema, until three generations, almost mad,
found one final diagnosis to explain

the rampant spread. We retreated to our homes,
spanning west to east, and basted itching skins.
It took weeks of tracking back: a log of everyone

we'd touched, human accounting,
until we came to Grandma, dead four months
and my sister's last visit at the hospital,

stroking the red, papery arms, then leaving
to gather up her son, and later, smooth
my baby daughter's belly, grip my hand on a beach.

Pleurisy v

My daughter
comes to sit beside me
and read.

I struggle
to complete a sentence
of praise,

head bent, blown.
She strokes my face,
a touch

that defines herself
as mine.
Her lungs expand

and she doesn't
feel them.
The breaths she makes

are clear and young.
She is
studying my fatigue.

This child,
inhaling the space
between us.

She is
present. She is
air.

Warren Street

I am not often jolted against you
and as my palm splays on the blue
of your shirt, I find myself very close to your face.

So close, that fellow passengers fall away
from my peripheral vision, and despite
having woken with you that morning

and knowing I will sleep with you tonight,
the carriage becomes an intimate space
and I feel privately in love with you,

so if people were to look up from their *Metros*
for a moment, see our reflections
in the doors, they would think there was something

very new between us just from the way
I was studying your profile, every fleck of white
in the beard that shapes your mouth. No matter

that my other husbands, your other wives
could be swaying in their seats
further down the train (we could so easily not

have met) but it is Tuesday afternoon, of which
I've spent a thousand in your company and this
might just be my pick, two hundred feet beneath
daylight, thinking how much I like that blue on you.

Something Beautiful Was
Created by Their Leaving

after Alison Watt, 'Sabine' (2000)

Let me amass
all the loved
of my life.

Draw them up
in this drapery
knotted

at my waist
to be carried
for long, selfish

distances.
Their breaths
warming

the folds
my fingers slip
between.

Let me know
mouths at my
knuckles.

I will return home
to undo
and open out.

To accept
the eventual
rising

of the loved.
I will
watch them

leave me,
free of my bed,
my grip,

their tender
weights still lovely
in the cloth.

Acknowledgements

Thanks are due to the editors of the following publications in which some of these poems, or versions of them, first appeared: *Agenda, Ambit, And Other Poems* (online), *Bare Fiction, Brittle Star, Disclaimer Magazine* (online) *IOTA, New Walk Magazine, Plume* (online), *Poems In Which* (online), *Poetry Review, The Compass* (online), *The Interpreter's House, The Learned Pig* (online), *The London Magazine* (online), *The Moth, The North, The White Review, Stand.*

'Betty Draper Shoots at Her Neighbour's Pigeons' first published in *Furies: A Poetry Anthology of Women Warriors,* ed. Eve Lacey, For Books' Sake, 2014

'Ants' first published in *Her Wings Of Glass,* (ed.) Myra Schneider, Penelope Shuttle and Dilys Wood, Second Light Publications, 2014. Highly Commended in the Mirehouse Poetry Competition, 2013

'White Currants' – Highly Commended in the Mirehouse Poetry Competition, 2014

'Ida and the Box' first published in *Other Countries: Contemporary Poets Rewiring History,* (ed.) Claire Trévien and Gareth Prior, Inpress, 2015

'Wet' – one of three poems commissioned by BBC Arts, for 'Body Language', BBC Taster, broadcast online, 2015

'The Lightning' – longlisted in the Mslexia Women's Poetry Competition, 2015

'The Baby Who Understood Shadows' – commissioned for and first published in *Writing Motherhood,* (ed.) Carolyn Jess-Cooke, Seren, 2017

'From Such Folds', 'Fabric', 'To Say Everything Is White' first published in *After Alison Watt,* The Triptych Series, Guillemot Press, 2017

'Something Beautiful Was Created by Their Leaving' – the poem's title comes from the artist Alison Watt, a phrase she has stated in several interviews, and is used here with her kind permission. Additional heartfelt thanks to Alison Watt for the use of her painting *Iris* as the cover of this book.

Thanks and gratitude to my editor, my husband, my parents and my girlfriends.